FIGHTERS AND FIGHTER BOMBERS

FIGHTERS AND FIGHTER BOMBERS

Octavio Díez

Author
Octavio Díez

Design and Layout
S. García and G. Ferré

Editorial Co-ordination
E. Marín

Editorial Project
2006 © UDYAT S.L.

ISBN: 84-933924-9-9
Legal deposit B-184-2006

Printed in Spain

FIGTHERS AND FIGHTER BOMBERS
INDEX

FIGHTER BOMBERS
OF THE XXI CENTURY

The long period of sustained growth of the aeronautical industry, the latest technologies and new military requirements have led to the development of a new generation of fighter planes that will enter service during the first two decades of the XXI century.

Dual origin

Two main groups lead the current military aeronautical market. The main power is concentrated in the United States, opposed by a Europe, whose international efforts are aimed at unifying their industry. The panorama is completed with Russian initiatives that contribute few novelties, and some specific projects in Asia using mostly American technology.

New requirements

The current projects of companies like Boeing or Lockheed Martin respond to the challenge of the American armed forces-and thus of those of other nations -of implementing new models of fighters and fighter bombers that are gradually replacing current models.

The new models of fighter bombers for the U.S. Air Force, Marines and the Navy are based on three options: the F-22 Raptor, which fulfills the need for a long-range stealth fighter with substantial combat capacity; the F-35 or JSF (Joint Strike Fighter) developed to serve all three services; and the F-18E Super Hornet, the future cornerstone of the American Navy's aircraft carriers. Their introduction into service will allow the gradual withdrawal of planes such as the F-4 Phantom, the F-15 Eagle, the F-16 Fighting Falcon and the AV-8 Harrier whose designs, although modernized, date from the 1960s and 70s.The renovation will begin with the oldest models and continue until, by 2025-2030, no current planes, including the F-117 will remain in service.

Shared thinking

Europe has similar requirements, with the difference that government initiatives have been added to private enterprise in order to dominate a sector considered strategic.

The main rivals are EADS (European Air Defense and Space Company) which groups together the Germans, British, Spaniards and Italians, and Dassault which leads the French effort.

The famous F-4 Phantom which was so successful in the Vietnam conflict continues to be used in some countries after much modernization.

The famous F-4 Phantom which was so successful in the Vietnam conflict continues to be used in some countries after much modernization.

Multi-role light fighters

The European proposals, which have received a boost from the need to renew the fleets of combat planes of the former Eastern Bloc countries, are centered on three models. The first is the EF-2000 Typhoon, of which about 620 will be built for the air forces of the four EADS countries. Greece has expressed an interest for some time and was negotiating an order for 90 planes, which was subsequently modified to 60 with an option for a further 30. The 2004 Olympic Games in Greece and the enormous government expenditure on infrastructures means the negoatiatons have been postponed until a later date. This plane, whose development has been slower than expected, will be a substantial improvement on the planes it replaces and ensures European control of all aspects of the technology.

The French, who first opted for shared European development and later decided on their own plan, are already delivering the first Rafale to the French navy and airforce. Its many advantages should ensure good sales in markets where French influence is strong, such as Asia and the Middle East.

The Swedish policy of independent development has resulted in the Gripen light fighter bomber, which has, however, needed some external technology. The commercial agreement that unites Saab, their maker, with British Aerospace has resulted in an unexpected success with firm contracts being signed with medium-sized countries.

Sometime around 2010, the new light reactor evolving from the German Mako design should come onto the market. Designed basically for advanced training missions, but capable of other actions, it has aroused interest in various countries including Spain. The new generation of Russian planes represent an effort to maintain a position in the world market and are primarily destined for export, given the financial problems besetting the former Soviet republics.

THE EUROPEAN
INDUSTRY

◄ *The Jaguar, a French-British attack plane was one the first examples of European aeronautical cooperation.*

► *The AMX an Italian light fast attack plane made under license by Brazil. Few countries can aspire to this level.*

Historical necessity has obliged European countries to join forces in search of a real economic and military union, although the latter objective is proving difficult. To achieve these goals agreements to cooperate industrially on large projects such as the EF-2000 fighter-bomber, the A-400M tactical transport plane the Meteor air-to-air missile have been signed.

A prosperous future

For Europe as a whole, it is vital to increase technological self-sufficiency compared with the giant American industry, their fiercest competitor in the world's military markets.

Technological leadership

Advances in aviation technology, which are also linked to other sectors of industry, require huge investment, such as that which has ensured that the radar, engines and electronic defense systems of the EF-2000 are overwhelmingly of European design.

Thus, on the one hand, there are Great Britain, Italy, Spain and Germany united in the EADS consortium, with a capacity for large-scale production. On the other hand, there is the

agreement linking Sweden and Britain in the development of the Gripen and the independent position maintained by France that, in the long run could prove to be more harmful than beneficial.

New markets

The gradual incorporation of the former Eastern bloc countries to the West's socio-economic system foreshadows the creation of a larger market.

These countries have already begun programs to acquire new generations of fighters which, through short-and medium-term alliances are intended to revolutionize their industry.

One example is Poland which has sold its

former manufacturer of transport planes to the Spanish EADS CASA company.

Commercial unity

In spite of the combined efforts - European programs for transport, attack and naval warfare helicopters are progressing satisfactorily - European interests are diverse and often opposed, as shown by the fact that various nations, including Italy and Turkey have opted for the American JSF.

Even so, the prospect of renewal of fleets is strong enough to be able to forecast the appearance of a new generation of attack and trainer aircraft during the next decade and a new fighter-bomber during the following one.

THE EF-2000 TYPHOON,
THE FUTURE EUROPEAN FIGHTER

The EF-2000 Typhoon – also known as the Eurofighter – will be the main fighter-bomber of the air forces of Germany, Spain, Italy and the United Kingdom for the first three decades of the XXI century.

Design philosophy

With special emphasis in their low-stress wings, the high propulsion/weight ration, minimal radar signature and optimally ergonomic cockpit, the one- and two-seat versions of the Typhoon fulfill the ESR-D requirements: a twin-engine supersonic plane with a delta-wing configuration and canards that allow combat maneuvers not possible with previous designs.

Advanced sensors

A third-generation multimode digital radar – developed by the Euroradar consortium comprising the British GEC Marconi, the Italian FIAR, the Spanish ENOSA of the INDRA group, and the German Telefunken Systemtechnik – operates by Doppler pulses and incorporates substantial advances in the antenna, transmitter and signal processor. In addition, there is an infrared search and guidance system and an electronic warfare DASS (Defensive Aids Sub-System) able to respond, automatically or manually to multiple threats.

It includes an ESM/ECM system, a radar alert detector of chaff and interceptor flare launching facilities.

All systems are controlled by an integrated avionics system which allows the pilot maximum management of both the flight and the tactical situation.

Flight control depends on Fly-By-Wire ACT (Active Control Technology)it Activates Control Technology)which uses various processors to regulate the inherent aerodynamic instability which give the plane high levels of maneuverability thanks to the two specifically-designed EJ 200 turbojets.

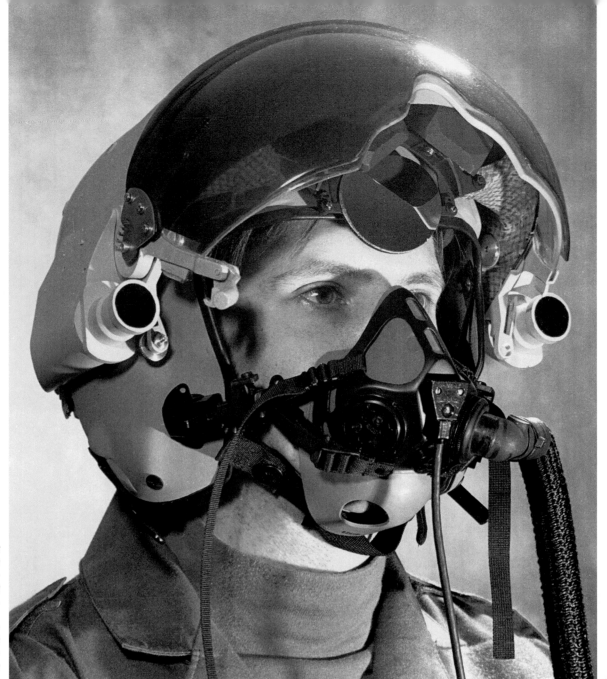

◀ *The process of joint development of the Typhoon promises continuing improvements during the coming decades.*

▶ *The helmet design incorporates advanced features which reduce the supportable working load and provide more information.*

Optimized cockpit

The cockpit includes Martin Baker MK16A ejector seat and three Multi-Function Head Down Displays (MHDDs) that show tactical data, the state of the various subsystems and lands maps combined with air traffic movements. A HUD (Head-Up Display) displays basic flight data, while the HMS (Helmet Mounted Symbology) incorporates of night-vision technology and optical protection.

The VTAS (Voice-Throttle-And-Stick) control facilitates high-intensity maneuvers. The control column has functions that control the sensors and weapons, defensive measures and the flight. The DVI (Direct Voice Input) permits verbal command of HUD and MHDD screens and the selection of targets and radio frequencies.

Armament

Thirteen anchorage points allow a maximum of 6.5 tons of armaments. In air-to-air actions the plane can carry 6 medium-range and radar-guided Meteor missiles or AMRAAM (Advanced Medium Range Air to Air Missile) in dedicated fuselage and underwing pods. Alternatively, 6 infrared-guided ASRAAM (Advanced Small Range Air to Air Missile) and a 27 mill Mauser gun can be carried.

The plane has 7 anchorage stations for free-falling air-to-ground bombs, autonomous

Brimstone systems, guided bombs, air-to-surface missiles, anti-ship weapons like the Harpoon and the Penguin, laser designators and various supplementary pods. It can also launch cruise missiles like the Storm Shadow.

Tested experience

The plane's versatility has aroused the interest of different air forces including Norway, Greece and Austria. The first planes from Tranche 1 were delivered during 2003 to the four participating countries.

There are firm orders for up to 620 more planes –100 of which are two-seats – which guarantees production up to 2014; 148 in

Tranche 1, 236 in Tranche 2 and the same number in Tranche 3, which is projected to incorporate improvements such as AESO radar and significant reductions in the radar section due to the use of RAM absorbent materials.

Also being evaluated is the option of a vectorial propulsion turbine, which, together with structural modifications would allow exceptional maneuverability.

The experience gained from this program will form the base of the new ETAP (European Technology Acquisition Program) which aims to manufacture 1000 airplanes with a new multi-role design which could include pilot-less planes.

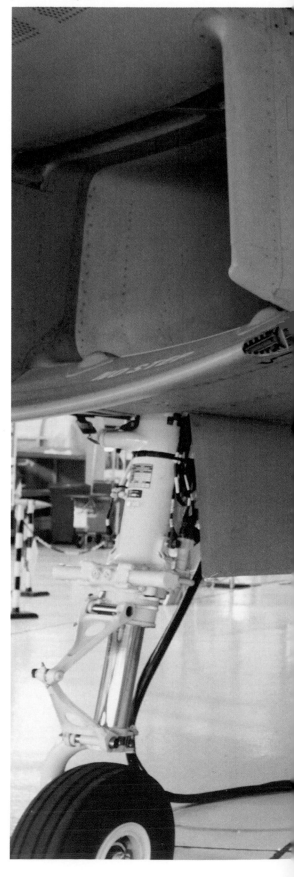

Technical characteristics: Tranche 1	
Cost (in millions of dollars):	70
Size:	
Length	15,96 m
Height	5,28 m
Wing span including missile launchers	10,95 m
Wing area	50 m²
Canard area	2,40 m²
Weight:	
Empty	10.995 Kg
Maximum	23.000 Kg
Maximum external load	6.500 Kg
Interior fuel	4.900 Kg
External fuel	4.500 Kg
Engines:	2 Turbofan Eurojet EJ 200 with 9.000 Kg of thrust each
Performance:	
Combat ceiling	15.000 m
High altitude speed	Mach 2
Low altitude speed	Mach 1
Take off requirement	700 m
Combat range	600 Km
Ferry range	3.000 Km
Design load factor	9 / -3 g´s

THE TORNADO,
THE EUROPEAN ATTACK PLANE

▶ *Detail of the two engines of this European attack plane able to fly with great accuracy at very low altitudes.*

Conceived to offset terrestrial threats from a large-scale attack to by the Warsaw Pact forces, the Tornado evolved toward the carrying out of air-to-air and air-to-surface missions in successive versions.

Multinational

The Tornado started life in the middle of the 1960s within the North Atlantic Treaty Organization (NATO), which wanted a plane able to carry out accurate attacks without being detected by enemy radar or shot down by anti-air systems. In July 1968, viability studies began in Italy, Germany, Great Britain, Belgium, Canada and the United States, although finally, only the first three countries continued with the project.

The first of the nine validation prototypes took off in August 1974. After agreeing a common manufacturing program participated in by a large number of companies led by British Aerospace, the German DASA and the Italian Alenia, a multinational training center was established at the Cottesmore RAF base.

Production

Deliveries to operational squadrons began in 1982. In 1989, coinciding with the decision to improve the British GR.1, the last of the IDS models were delivered to Italy and Germany. In January 1992, the last of the German ECRs was produced and in November of the same year production for the RAF finished. In the following five years, the British industry fulfilled a contract with Saudi Arbia in addition to that agreed during the middle of the previous decade.

Currently, the German planes are undergoing a MLU (Mid Life Update) which includes new avionics and new equipment such as the pods of the Rafael laser designator or the FLIR infrared designator. The Italian planes will undergo similar improvements.

One of the latest improvements has been the incorporation of the RAPTOR pod in the British Tornados to provide both day and night laser-guided bombing facilities. The planes, which will have an accuracy of less than three meters, should be operational at the end of 2003, coinciding with the completion of improvements to 142 GR4s which should prolong their operational life until 2020.

Specialized

Flying at 540 knots and at less than 200 feet,

▼ The Tornado's performance means it is viable until 2020, but some countries will probably retire it from service before then.

▼ The Tornado's performance means it is viable until 2020, but some countries will probably retire it from service before then.

formations of British Tornados armed with JP233 submunition launchers began attacking Iraqi airbases on the night of January 17 1991 as part of the international Desert Storm operation, which sustained heavy losses among the attacking forces due to saturation of weapons and defensive missile systems. However, the Tornado IDS demonstrated an optimal penetration capacity thanks to the ability of varying its wing arrows according to the speed and height of the flight.

Attack and defense

The most advanced variant of the IDS model is the British GR.4 whose profile makes detection very difficult.

The pilot is supported by a holographic HUD system that allows the super-positioning of FLIR images. In addition, the modified avionics are compatible with the use of third-generation night-glasses and configured with multi-role screens which provide digital information on flight plans and systems performance, as well as the accuracy of modern GPS systems.

The copilot is in command of the designation, which can launch guided bombs from a safe distance, while controlling the electronic countermeasures activated by the Marconi Zeus radar system.

The ADV variant, currently being upgraded, includes systems such as AWS, ADMS and SPILS which optimize its performance as an aerial defense plane and includes reinforced absorbent panels to reduce the radar signature. The plane uses a Marconi Foxfighter Doppler radar which includes an IFF interrogator and can detect objectives at up to 185 km.

Offensive

With an external cargo load of more than 8 tons, the IDS variant carries two 27 mm Mauser guns, the MW-1 and JP233 submu-

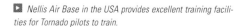 The German Navy uses these planes in a specialized configuration for naval missions, arming them with Kormoran missiles.

▶ Nellis Air Base in the USA provides excellent training facilities for Tornado pilots to train.

nitions launchers, laser Paveway and BL755 submunition bombs, AGM-65 Maverick guided missiles, Eagle and Kormoran anti-ship missiles, rocket launchers, and free-fall bombs. The defensive systems include two AIM-9 Sidewinder missiles and ASRAAM. The ADV is armed with a single 27 mm gun, Sidewinders and 6 medium-range Hughes AIM-120 AMRAAM missiles. The ECR nor-mally includes pods of electronic counter-measures, interference flares, Harm anti-radiation missiles and auxiliary fuel tanks.

Powerful

The attack model is equipped with two turbo-fan Turbo-union RB199-34R engines, which in the Mk103 variant, produce a propulsion of 6,750 kg per unit, guaranteeing problem-free low-altitude flight where performance is enhanced by the automatic contour-fol-lowing equipment which combines radar and intertial navigation.

The air defense model includes two Mk104 turbofans with 6.940 kg of propulsion per unit, while the CR of electronic warfare includes the Mk105 version of the RB199 which improves propulsion by ten per cent.

Model	Purchasers	Year	Mission
IDS	Germany, Italy and Saudi Arabia	1982	All-weather fighter-bomber
IDS	Germany navy	1982	Anti-ship and area reconnaissance
ECR	Germany and Italy	1990	Electronic warfare and reconnaissance
GR1	United Kingdom	1982	All-weather fighter-bomber
GR1A	United Kingdom	1987	All-weather tactical reconnaissance
GR4	United Kingdom	2000	All-weather fighter-bomber with enhance night-flying capabilities
GR4A	United Kingdom	2001	All-weather tactical reconnaissance with real-time data transmission capabilities
ADV Mk3	United Kingdom and Saudi Arabia	1986	All-weather interceptor, air superiority fighter, combat patrol plane

Characteristics

	Variant IDS	Variant ADV
Cost (in millions of dollars):	35	42
Size:		
Length	16,70 m	18,10 m
Height	5,95 m	5,95 m
Wingspan maximum extension	8,60 m	8,60 m
Wingspan minimum extension	13,91 m	13,91 m
Wing area	26,60 m²	26,60 m²
Weight:		
Empty	13.890 Kg	14.500 Kg
Maximum	27.950 Kg	27.986 Kg
Maximum external load	9.000 Kg	8.500 Kg
Internal fuel	5.830 l	6.580 l
External fuel	4.500 l	4.500 l
Engines:	2 turbofan Turbo-Union RB199-34R Mk103 with a unit thrust of 6,750 kg	2 turbofan Turbo-Union RB199-34R Mk104 with a unit thrust of 6,940 kg
Performance:		
Ceiling	15.000 m	15.000 m
High-altitude speed	Mach 2,2	Mach 2,2
Low-altitude speed	Mach 1,22	Mach 1,22
Take off requirement	900 m	700 m
Combat range	1.390 Km	1.390 Km
Ferry range	3.890 Km	3.890 Km
Design load factor	7,5 g's	7,5 g's

RAFALE
INDEPENDENCE AND CAPACITY

◀ The Rafale demonstrates the desire of France to maintain their independence in defense matters.

▶ The new integrated sensors improve performance and provide more information to the pilot on possible targets.

In spite of the initial French involvement in the development of the European fighter-bomber, the ECA, pressure from the influential French defense industry, the government's consistent policy of independence and the need for a spearheading export product which could reactivate other sectors led to the decision to opt for a purely national project which would include both a two-seat tactical attack plane and a multi-role single-seat interceptor.

Prototypes

While collaborating in the conception of the ECA, Dassault continued developing its own new fighter-bomber. The first prototype of the Rafale A took off in July 1986, although it used American General Electric F404 engines-those used in the F-18 – as the French SNECMA M88 would not be ready until February 1990.

Testing

The model C single-seat began operational flights in October 1991 and the M, the naval model, in December of the same year, after extensive testing which included catapult launches at the Patuxent River Base in the USA and landings on the Foch aircraft carrier. In February 1993 a two-seat prototype began flights, equipped with the Thomson-CSF/Dassault Electronique RBE2 (Radar à Bayalage Electronique) system and the Spectra defensive system.

Forecasts

The initial idea was to sell around five hundred planes in various markets. However, to date, the only planes in operation are those of the French Air Force and Navy, who, due to budget

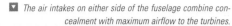
cuts, have reduced their expected orders to 234 and 60 planes, respectively.

The model M planes – F1 standard – were the first delivered to the nuclear aircraft carrier Charles de Gaulle. Some were deployed on the 12F Fleet during the Afghanistan campaign in 2001-2002, although more for purposes of evaluation than for effective participation.

The French air force has also received two biplanes, the B301 and B302, part of the 36 planes ordered, which will be delivered by 2010.

Operations

The operational configuration of the Rafale can be changed rapidly and the plane can execute day and night missions in all weather conditions. Short – and medium – range capabilities include ground attack, defense and air superiority, scouting and precise attacks, using both conventional and nuclear weapons, with the RBE2 radar capable of acquiring up to 8 targets.

Integration

The Rafale multi-role light fighter is equipped with processors which allow the pilot to control most systems with the HOTAS (Hands on Throttle And Stick) control column. Equipped with an ILS (Integrated Logistic Support), its efficient aerodynamics incorporate various refinements that reduce the radar signature considerably.

Advanced

The mission computers control all parameters relating to the flight, engines, tactical sensors, plan of action, defense systems, life-support, navigation and data links. Integration between pilot and plane is improved by the position of the pilot's seat, the OBOGS autonomous oxygen system, the high-definition multicolor screens, the SEMMB Mk16 ejector seat reclined at an angle of 29°, and the visor integrated in the helmet.

Control

A digital flight control system guarantees natural stabilization in three axes and safe piloting due to the automatic flight control and associated features such as the auto-pilot, the altimeter or the inertial guidance system. These characteristics, combined with the power of the two SNECMA M88 modular engines, which although smaller and lighter than other conventional designs, offer a high thrust/weight ratio and can carry out long-range missions without restrictions. The plane combines a high level of autonomy, with low consumption and reduced maintenance costs.

Technical Characteristics model C	
Cost (in millions of dollars):	45
Size:	
Length	15,30 m
Height	5,30 m
Wingspan	10,80 m
Wing area	45,70 m²
Weight:	
Empty	10.000 Kg
Maximum	24.500 Kg
Maximum external load	9.500 Kg
Internal fuel	4.500 Kg
External fuel	7.500 Kg
Engines:	Two SNECMA M-88-2 engines with a combined thrust of 13,800 kg
Performance:	
Ceiling	18.000 m
High-altutide speed	Mach 1,8
Low-altitude speed	Mach 1
Take-off requirement	450 m
Combat range	1.852 Km
Ferry range	4.000 Km
Design load factor	9 g's

▼ *The robustness of the front landing gear allows landings and takeoffs from aircraft carriers.*

▼ *Part of the electronic warfare equipment is housed in this pod in the tail unit, to avoid interfering with others located in the fuselage.*

▲ These Rafale have been adapted for use at sea and will be deployed on the French nuclear aircraft carrier Charles of Gaulle.

▼ Thirty multi-role Rafale make up the squadrons assigned to the French aircraft carriers.

MIRAGE 2000,
THE LATEST FRENCH DELTA

The Mirage 2000 follows on from the Mirage III and F1 fighters and was proposed as a cheaper alternative to the cancelled ACF (Avion du Combat Futur) project. Their sales have maintained France as the third most-important exporter of weapons in the world.

Development

Manufactured by Dassault Aviation, the inaugural flight of the Mirage 2000 took place at the Istres Base on March 10 1976. A specific variant with nuclear penetration capacities became operational in February 1983 and in October 1990 the multi-role 2000-5 was unveiled.

Deliveries

The first 22 planes were bought by the French defense ministry in 1980. The first squadron exported became operational in 1985. Eight countries, including the United Arab Emirates, Qatar and Taiwan, have ordered almost six hundred planes, and production is expected to continue until 2005.

Multi-role

Initially conceived as an interceptor, the Mirage 2000, has been adapted successfully for multiple combat activities including long-range interception, air defense and supe-

The Mirage 2000-5 has RDY radar, and the navigation and enhanced attack systems or the integrated countermeasures are characteristic.

The data screens of the cockpit of the Mirage 2000 are more comprehensive than older versions and include the most modern technology.

riority, long-range penetration, attacks on strategic targets, airbase neutralization using anti-runway weapons, naval traffic control, reconnaissance and tactical and strategic nuclear attack.

Development

The first models included Thomsom-CSF RDM multi-mode radar and later ones the Dassault Electronique/Thomson-CSF Doppler RDI, both systems having an estimated reach of 100 km and able to operate in areas saturated with electronic countermeasures.

Equipment

The pilot is seated in a Martin-Baker F-10Q ejector seat, manufactured in France under license. The plane has a Fly-by Wire flight control system, an SFENA auto-pilot and ABG-Semca air conditioning in the advanced cockpit.

Propulsion

The plane's engine is a SNECMA M53-P2 turbofan, with superb acceleration, which can fly at around Mach 1 at low altitude and more than Mach 2 at high altitude, with a thrust of 9,690 kg with fuel, rising to 9,900 in the P20 variant, and 6,500kg with empty tanks.

Weapons

The Mirage 2000's armory includes free-falling 250kg bombs, 1,000 kg laser-guided bombs, Durandal and BAP 100 anti-runway bombs, Belouga submunitions dispensers, APACHE long-range cruise missiles, laser-guided high-precision AS30L missiles, Armat anti-radar missiles, AM39 Exocet anti-ship missiles and, in the N variety with nuclear penetration, the ASMP with a nuclear warhead.

Mirage 2000-5

The first French models became operational on February 26, 1996. Recently, Brazil has undertaken a lengthy evaluation of the plane with the possible purchase of around twenty planes, planned to be the first of approximately one hundred, although recent political developments has affected the programme.

Multi-role

The Mirage 2000-5 is a multi-role fighter, principally with air-to-air capabilities. It is equipped with a Thomson-CSF RDY multi-mode radar able to detect 24 targets simultaneously and engage the 8 most-hostile ones. It is also equipped with the ICMS integrated system of electronic countermeasures which needs no external pods. The cockpit contains a HUD/HLD visor, a HD visor in which the pilot can check the tactical situation, two lateral data presentation screens, and a central screen showing radar and HOTAS flight control data.

Technical Characteristics 2.000C	
Cost (in millions of dollar):	34,5
Size:	
Length	14,16 m
Height	5,20 m
Wingspan	9,13 m
Wing area	41,00 m²
Weight:	
Empty	7.500 Kg
Maximum	17.000 Kg
Maximum external load	6.300 Kg
Internal fuel	3.978 Kg
External fuel	4.700 Kg
Engine:	One SNECMA M53-P2 turbofan with 9,690 kg of thrust
Performance:	
Ceiling	16.460 m
High-altitude speed	Mach 2,2
Low -altitude speed	Mach 0,9
Approach speed	259 Km/h
Take-off requirement	457 m
Combat range	1.480 Km
Ferry range	3.333 Km
Design load factor	9 g's

LOOKING
FOR NEW MARKETS

The disintegration of the USSR resulted in a budgetary shortage that has affected the Russian Air force and those of its neighbors. The post-Soviet aerospace industries have been forced to look to new export clients like China or India whose important orders, mainly for Sukhoi planes, have alleviated the crisis in the sector.

Future projects

While export-generated revenues allow for gradual future planning, attempts to expand in Latin-American markets such as Brazil and Chile have been hampered by economic recession or scandals such as the Peruvian MiG-29 affair. Nevertheless, new and highly competitive developments are now competing with Western companies, often with the added attraction of generous deals on modern weaponry which is included with the planes.

Domestic market

In forthcoming years, Russia will begin acquiring the latest generation of new fighter-bombers and upgrading some operational aircraft, although problems such as the lack of fuel or spare parts and deficient pilot training remain.

The injection of funds from the United States and Europe as a consequence of political agreements and the destruction of nuclear arsenals will improve the panorama. Meanwhile, work is underway on a fighter with stealth capabilities, meant to be an answer to the American Raptor and the European EF-2000, although it will not be operational until the end of the decade.

Changing forecasts

European and American consortia have been sounded out, but already have a large part of their production covered by domestic markets. Some Asian and African countries, traditional clients of the old USSR have been more receptive. Opportunism has proved to be the best policy. To counter purely technical criteria, the Russians are taking advantage of political and economic factors that condition the purchasing policies of many governments. A good example is the restrictions imposed by some Western states on countries considered hostile.

▲ Italy and Brazil have decided on intermediate, less expensive solutions, such as the AMX.

▶ Globally, there are many planes whose flying life is nearly at an end. The Spanish F-5B, in spite of modernization, cannot continuing flying after 2010-2015.

◀ The Czech Republic has developed the L-159, a variant of a trainer-reactor capable of defense and of attacking terrestrial and naval targets

SUKHOI,
THE LASTEST GENERATION

The Russian answer to Western advances in combat aircraft is now underway. The latest models from the Sukhoi factory score high marks for design, capacity and maneuverability and are highly sophisticated.

Entrepreneurial initiatives

The establishment, at the end of 2001, of the JSC Sukhoi Aviaton Holding company, gave the Russian firm the independence to renew its export tradition that began with the Su-15, Su-17, Su-20 and Su-22, which were sold to countries such as Afghanistan, Syria, Angola , Czechoslovakia, Algeria, Egypt, Poland, Syria, the Yemen and Vietnam.

These successes encouraged the development of a new attack plane, whose operational versions are known as the Su-19 Fencer and the Su-24 Fencer B. More than 900 of these planes have been built at the Komsomolsk plant. Their ability to take out terrestrial targets at low-altitude flight led to the development of the M variant, with terrain-following radar, the MR reconnaissance and electronic warfare plane and the MP electronic countermeasures plane, which came into service in the 1980s.

Light attack

The Su-25 Frogfoot, which saw action in the Afghanistan War is a small plane ideal for short-range support and infantry attack. The Su-25T anti-tank plane appeared in 1991 and has since been replaced by the Su-39 twin-engine light attack plane, which has an integrated navigation and firing system.

Interceptors

Known as the Ram-J until its detection by American spy planes, the Su-27 Flanker typified Russian potential in high-performance interceptors.

The first designs were made by Pavel Sukhoi in 1969 and the first flight was in 1981. The latest variant is the Su-27UBM, with a high maximum speed, various types of air-to-air missiles and a range of action of around 1,500 km.

Another derivation is the twin-seat, all-weather Su-30K fighter, which has a Doppler radar capable of detecting up to 10 targets at a range of 100 km and an optronic, infrared firing control system.

◀ *An example of the Russian industry's attempts to regain its former power is this plane, adapted to operate from aircraft carriers.*

▼ *The cockpit of the Su-32 houses both the pilot and the gunner.*

Offering more models

The need for new models to guarantee the company's future has led it to turn to other types of planes in order to widen its market.

Naval

The long-range, naval attack plane, the twin-seat Su-32FN, has an armored cockpit for the pilot and gunner. The wide span between the two engines gives better aerodynamics and the two-wheeled front landing gear allows it to operate from emergency landing strips. Originally known as the Su-27IB, and shown at the Le Bourget air show in 1995 and 1997, the plane is designed to attack naval targets including submarines and surface ships. Its

development has been delayed and the plane will not become operational until 2004.

The Future

One of the company's most important future projects is the Su-35, a multi-role advanced variant of the Flanker with vectorial thrust. Another is the experimental Su-37, capable of acquiring for air and surface targets simultaneously and which can carry R-37 and KS-172 air-to-air missiles, X-15P air-to-surface missiles and the X-65S stealth missile. At the 1997 Paris Air Show the company displayed a model of a new light fighter, a smaller version of the Su-35, intended

to the be the Russian answer to the demands of the coming century in terms of agility, combat power and performance. The specifications include canards, a double vertical rudder, a ventral Saturn AL-31F engine and Sokol Falcon fire-control radar with a maximum range of 180 km and which can engage four of the twenty-four targets acquired. The fifth-generation fighter S-37 Berkut, with its swept-back wings, canards and D-30F6 turbojets with vectorial thrust, is the latest current project from the resurgent Sukhoi company, making its maiden test flight in September 1997 at the Zhukovsky Testing Center.

► The multi-role performance of the Su-30Mk fighter-bomber is comparable to that of its Western equivalents.

▼ The Flanker is still enjoying some commercial success, notably the recent sales to China.

Technical Characteristics: Su-32FN	
Cost (in millions of dollar):	50 (estimated)
Size:	
Length	23,3 m
Height	6,5 m
Wingspan	14,7 m
Wing area	62,00 m²
Weight:	
Maximum	44.360 Kg
Maximum external load	8.000 Kg
Engine:	2 AL-31F turbofans with a unit thrust of 12.500 kg with afterburners and 7,500 kg without
Performance:	
Ceiling	18.000 m
High-altitude speed	Mach 1,8
Low-altitude speed	Mach 1,14
Ferry range	4.000 Km
Design load factor	9 g's

THE MiG-29 FULCRUM
RUSSIAN SUCCESS

◀ *Siting the air intakes in a low position favors air-flow to the turbines, although at the risk of sucking up foreign bodies.*

▶ *The MiG-29's technology dates from the 1980s and is now out-of-date, although improvements are being made, above all in the avionics.*

The single-seat MIG-29 fighter-bomber was the greatest Soviet challenge to American hegemony and continues to be a key product, at least in export terms.

Adapted

The first of 13 prototypes took off from the Ramenskoye Base on October 6 1977 and was observed by American spy planes the following month. In the West it was given the name RAM-L.

Service

The Fulcrum A- project 9.12- was the first variant produced, of which there were 3 subtypes, distinguished by small external details. The B model – project 9-51- is a combat-ready two-seat trainer, although lacking radar. After its first flight on May 4 1984, work began on the C model with improved cockpit-fuselage integration, allowing it to carry more electronic equipment.

Aircraft carriers

The Korabelny, or K model, began production in November 1989, specifically for use on aircraft carriers, with its performance being evaluated onboard the then-named Tiblisi. The ends of its wings are retractable and the plane is equipped with a Zhuk radar and special RD-22K engines. The K has a greater fuel capacity and can carry various types of weapons including the anti-ship AS- 17 Krypton missiles. The two-seat variant is known as the KUB.

Exports

The type S has evolved from the type C from 1982 onwards, mainly with a view to improving exports. This type includes the SD, SE, SM and SMT models, equipped with a more modern N0 19 (RP- 29) Sapfire radar capable of engaging two fighters simultaneously.

The SD bought by Malaysia and designated there the MIG-29N, include adaptations for use in tropical climates and structural improvements which allow a 28° angle of attack compared to the original 22°.

Other variants include the two-seat M2, adapted for ground attacks, and the OVT, equipped with an experimental engine with vectorial thrust. The latest clients include Iran and Yemen.

Improvements

At the 1997 Le Bourget air show, new specifications were presented, including improved avionics, and N019M Topaz radar, whose terrain-following capacities give it a resolution of 15 m.

During 2002, the Hungarian air force undertook the modernization of 14 planes which, thanks to the adoption of systems compatible with those used by NATO forces, will remain on active service until the next decade. In the same year, Bulgaria also decided on the modernization of its fleet by the Russian comapany RSK MiG In addition,

Poland has sought to buy the 29 MiG-29G/GT used until now by Germany, with the aim of keeping 20 on active service and using the rest for spare parts.

Successful sales

Initially built at the Znamya Truda and Nizhny Novgorod factories under the auspices of the Moscow Aircraft Production Organisation (MAPO), some 1500 planes have been produced, of which around 200 are two-seat UB. Apart from the 800 destined for the Russian air force, around 500 planes have been exported to almost 30 countries, including, it is believed Israel, which managed to acquire some for dissimilar training and the United States, which, during the last years of the XX century bought 21 planes from Moldavia.

Controversies

Peru has also bought some second-hand planes from Belorussia and new ones from Russia, but these deals have been involved in a political scandal due to various accidents. What is sure is that the planes are equipped with long-range air-to-air missiles, the only ones in Latin America.

Combat

During the Gulf War, various Iraqi planes of this type fought against Western opposition, with the loss of many planes. In Bosnia too, the plane was not successful, although this may be due more to inadequate pilot training rather than the planes themselves. However, the plane can carry a wide and powerful range of weapons, including a gun, bombs and various missiles, supported by the infrared OEPS-29 seeker, which has a range of 15 km and is installed in front of the cockpit and the Doppler RLS RP-29 radar which can acquire and engage targets flying at lower altitudes within a radius of 100 km and is collimated with a laser telemeter. In spite of its specifications, German pilots have reported a lack of power and complicated handling.

These large vertical rudders on the tail help to stabilize the plane and give it a rather strange shape.

Technical Characteristics variant C	
Cost (in million of dollars):	28
Size:	
Length	17,32 m
Height	4,73 m
Wingspan	11,36 m
Wing area	38,00 m²
Weight:	
Empty	10.900 Kg
Maximum	18.500 Kg
Maximum external load	3.000 Kg
Internal fuel	4.500 Kg
External fuel	2.200 Kg
Engines:	2 Klimov/Sarkisov RD-33 turbofans with 8,290 kg of unit thrust.
Performance:	
Ceiling	17.000 m
High-altitude speed	Mach 2,3
Low-altitude speed	Mach 1,06
Take-off requirement	250 m
Combat range	600 Km
Ferry range	2.900 Km
Designload factor	9 g's

THE JAS-39 GRIPEN
THE SWEDISH INITIATIVE

Proud of their independence in all ways, Sweden has traditionally also been self-sufficient in defense matters. This policy is reflected in the successes of their competitive aeronautical industry, which include the Saab 35 Draken, the various models of the Saab 37 Viggen and the JAS 39 (Jakt Attack Spaning)attack and reconnaissance fighter.

Project

Named after the mythological Griffin, an ambitious project began in June 1980 to conceive, design and produce a light combat aircraft incorporating the latest technological advances and capable of operating independently from temporary landing sites such

as selected sections of motorways and even some urban streets.

Requirements

After rejecting various foreign options that did not meet the demanding operational objectives, a development contract was signed between the JAS industrial group and the Swedish Defense Ministry for five prototypes and 30 production models.

The program was confirmed in the spring of 1983, with encouraging initial which fulfilled the agreed schedule, culminating in the flight of the first prototype on December 9 1988. However, soon after, due to problems in the management of the digital system, the prototype suffered two accidents, being destroyed on the second occasion on February 2 1989, resulting in a temporary halt in the program.

Testing

Foreign expertise – mainly American – was sought in order to solve the problem of deficient software and other problems with the fuel system, the integrated starter, and the refrigeration of the avionics, while, at the same time, a two-seat model was in development.

The four remaining prototypes first flew between May 1990 and October 1991.

On June 3, 1992, an order was approved for 110 models from batch 2, which would include enhanced software, a new flight-control system, provision for a TARAS communications system, updated processors and even different camouflage.

Production

The first production model became operational on September 10 1992, with the first

▶ *The JAS-39 is considered as the first fourth-generation fighter.*

◀ *In the future, the Gripen will be able to operate with Meteor missiles designed to hit long-distance aerial targets.*

30 operational models being delivered at the end of 1996 and the first two-seater delivered in April of the same year. In June 1997 the Swedish government announced the purchase of 64 new JAS 39 from batch 3 which will include technological advances such as improved turbines. In September 1997 the Wing F7 Squadron, stationed at the Satenas Base, became operational.

Multi-role

The JAS 39 was conceived with specific performance criteria in order to guarantee the highest level of autonomy. This has resulted in qualities ideal for modern aerial combat, with the plane being very successful as a medium-range interceptor or anti-ship plane, and can carry out accurate attacks both in support of ground forces or to destroy enemy targets.

Multinational

Although Swedish companies have carried out the bulk of the work, without the significant contributions of companies from the United States, United Kingdom, Germany, Hungary and France, the project would never have got off the ground.

Midway through 1995, an agreement was signed between Saab and British Aerospace - which already participated in the design and production of the wings at the beginning of the project – to promote an export model of the Gripen. The model is available in different configurations, including different engines, to avoid possible USA embargoes.

Advanced

Described as the first fourth-generation fighter to see service, the Gripen is notable for its easy maintenance and operative qualities.

The PS-05/A multi-mode Doppler radar is a collaboration between Ericsson Radio and Ferranti. The carbon fiber antenna incorporates search functions for terrestrial, aerial and naval targets. Forty processors manage the flight parameters, the HOTAS control system and the HUD visor with diffractive optics, as well as the conventional control column designed by Page Engineering of the UK and equipped with artificial contact. The ejector seat is a Martin Baker S10LS.

Single engine

Although based on the General Electric F404 turbofan, Aero Volvo and Saab have developed an improved model designated as the RM12, which can reach Mach 1.08 without afterburners.

Contacts have begun with the German company Dasa and the American consortium Boeing/Rockwell International to develop a variant of the RB12 engine with TVC (Trust Vector Control) aimed mainly at the export market. This change needs an adapted flight control, complicates the system, adds weight and increases the cost, but offers greater maneuverability, more angles of attack without losing height and lower speed landing These significant advantages have resulted in contracts being signed with South Africa, Hungary and the Czech Republic. Sweden aims to keep improving the JAS 39 Gripen so that it will still be flying by the year 2040.

Cost (in millions of dollars):	50 including development
Size:	
Length	14,10 m
Height	4,50 m
Wingspan	8,40 m
Weight:	
Empty	6.622 Kg
Maximum	13.000 Kg
Maximum external load	3-4 t
Internal fuel	2.268 Kg
External fuel	2.000 Kg
Engines:	One RM12 with 8,165 kg of thrust
Performance:	
Ceiling	15.000 m
High-altitude speed	Mach 1,8
Low-altitude speed	Mach 1,08
Take-off requirement	800 m
Combat range	3.000 Km
Design load factor	9 g's

THE HARRIER
VERTICAL TAKE OFF AND LANDING

◀ *The Sea Harriers earned their fame during the Falklands Wars.*

▶ *Despite the excellent performance of the latest generation of Harriers, they are due to be substituted after 2010.*

The Harrier was conceived for vertical take off and landing, made possible by vectoring the gases of the turbine outlet. It can operate from many sites, from small aircraft carriers to clearings in the forest. It proved its worth conclusively during the 1991 Gulf War.

Conception

In 1957 the British firm Hawker Siddeley conceived the idea of a military aircraft able to take off and land from small areas, and enlisted the collaboration of the Bristol Engine company, which specialized in advanced engines.

Kestrel

The initial project (Project 1127) was tested in static flight, tied to the ground with steel cables, at the end of September 1960. The results encouraged the British, Americans and Germans to form a tripartite evaluation squadron of nine P.1127 Kestrels. Once the idea and its possibilities had been confirmed, the RAF ordered the pre-production models,

designated as the Harrier, which were followed by the first GR Mk1 ground attack
and reconnaissance models, with deliveries
beginning in 1967.

Evolution

After the configuration of the T Mk.2 model
as a two-seat trainer, improvements were
made to the engines, leading to the Mk.1A
and Mk.2A with Pegasus 102 turbines. In 1971,
the first planes were delivered to the United
States Marine Corps with the designation of
AV-8A Alpha for the single-seat and TAV-8A
for the two-seat. Soon afterwards, the British
Mk.3 and T Mk.4 models which included a
laser designador in a lengthened radome and
passive threat-detector radar in the upper

part of the tail rudder,and were later on provided with the Pegasus 103 turbines.

In November 1972, the Spanish Navy purchased 12 single-seater and two-seaters
of the A Matador model, which remained
in service until they were re-exported to
Thailand in 1996.

Onboard

While the Marines were incorporating the AV-
8A, the Royal Navy was doing the same with
the naval model, the Harrier FRS1, with the
first planes being delivered in June 1979. Their
success in the Falklands War in 1982, in which
the various models of Harrier deployed shot
down two-thirds of the hundred Argentine
aircraft destroyed, provided welcome atten-

tion and resulted in a contract with the Indian
navy for 23 Sea Harrier Mk.51 for the Viraat
and Vikrant aircraft carriers.

Advanced

In 1984, deliveries began to the USMC of
the McDonnell Douglas AV-8B Bravo and
TAV-8B that, among other advances, had
redesigned wings and a front designator for
the launching of precision bombs.

 The model was adopted as the Mk.5 by the
RAF in 1987, with Spain acquiring 12 planes
the same year. In addition, the prototype of
the Night Attack model, which incorporated
an infrared sensor was successfully tested.
The Marines incorporated them immediate-
ly and the British reconverted their Mk.5

planes, designating them as the Mk.7.
In 1990, the British Sea Harriers were upgraded to the F/A2 model which incorporated the new GEC-Marconi Blue Vixen radar system. Soon afterwards, the USA, Spain and Italy ordered the new AV-8B+ or Plus, equipped with Hughes AN/APG-65 radar.
Deliveries began in 1993 combined with the upgrading of some batches from the B series to the new standard. The Marines purchased 27, the Italian navy 16 and the Spanish navy 8. At the end of 2001, Taiwanese interest, which could result in an order for 30 planes, to be delivered from 2005 onwards, was revealed.

Plus

Operating from air bases, temporary landing sites, amphibious vessels or small aircraft carriers, the Harrier has proved time and again its capacity to carry out many types of missions.

Propulsion

This adaptation to multiple scenarios is based on a Rolls-Royce F402-RR-408 Pegasus 11-61 turbine producing 9,000 kg of thrust and including four engine flow deflectors which provide maximum maneuverability for close-quarter fighting.

Configuration

Designed for a useful life of about 6,000 hours, the plane incorporates new features such as the thick wings of carbon fiber composite which give it greater lift and greater fuel-carrying capacity, ventral fins that replace the gun turret when this is not used or large admission nozzles that improve the cruising speed and optimize the short take off and landing capacity.

Equipment

The cockpit is equipped with a Martin Baker ejector seat. Air space and ground activity is controlled with a Hughes AN/APG-65 multi-mode Doppler radar (also used in the F-18A Hornet), which facilitates all-weather operations and is complemented by infrared illumination for night flights.
The AV-8B+ is equipped with a Smiths Industries HUD/HDD compatible with the use of night glasses, highly-accurate inertial navigation, communications systems which are resistant to electronic countermeasures, a digital color map screen, and defense measures which include interference cartridges, a threat screen and advanced jamming systems.

Technical Characteristics: AV-8B Plus	
Cost (in millions of dollars):	50
Size:	
Length	14,55 m
Height	3,55 m
Winspan	9,25 m
Wing area	21,37 m²
Weight:	
Empty	6.740 Kg
Maximum	14.061 Kg
Maximum external load	6.000 Kg
Internal fuel	4.600 l
External fuel	4.800 l
Performance:	
High-altitude speed	Mach 0,98
Low-altitude speed	Mach 0,87
Combat range	1.100 Km
Ferry range	3.641 Km
Design load factor	7 g's

THE AMERICAN
INDUSTRY

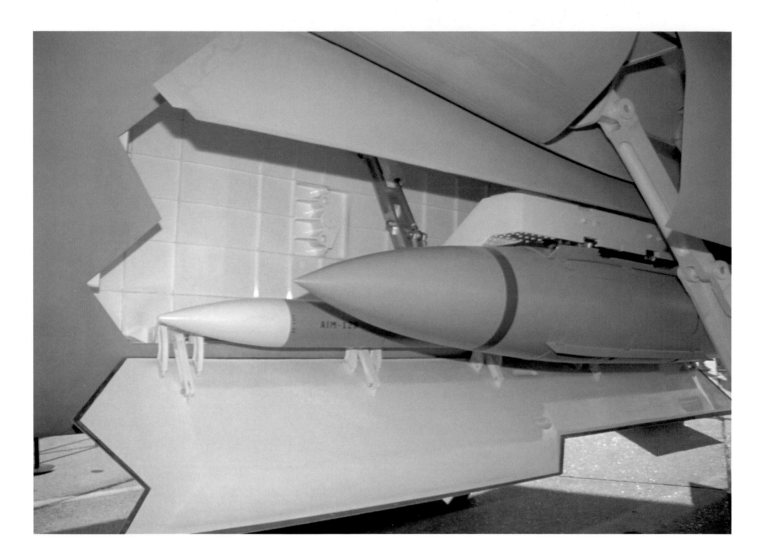

The United States is the undoubted leader in aeronautical development and its combat aircraft have few rivals. Home demand and the desire of the US. Air Force and Navy to always have the latest technology have resulted in a formidable industry which employs hundreds of thousands of workers. High research budgets help to maintain developments which, in turn, often result in benefits for other sectors of the economy.

Maintaining production

The Americans have maintained an intensive export policy, due not only to the profits generated by each individual package – which includes the planes, weapons, spares and even logistic support for the life of the plane – but also to offset development costs. However, the government's right of veto means that the US can help their allies, assure the peace in troubled regions and even, in some cases, destabilize perceived enemies. Sales are a double-edged sword,

which, occasionally has been used against American interests.

Traditional markets

Europe has been one of the most assiduous purchasers of the F-16 Fighting Falcon, the F-18 Hornet and the AV-8B Harrier II from American producers who consider this market to be essential in the short – and medium-term. Currently, the former Soviet Block countries are being tempted to buy on advantageous terms. The decision of some

countries to join the JSF program is a blow to European unity, at least insofar as military aircraft are concerned. The US is also very active in the Middle Eastern market, supplying both the Israelis, with the F-15 Eagle and the F-16, and other countries in the region, as shown by the recent contract with the United Arab Emirates.

Future prospects

Several Latin American countries have expressed an interest in renewing their out-

▲ With the introduction of a new version of the Hornet – seen here dressed in aggressive camouflage to simulate an enemy plane – production of the aircraft is assured for years to come.

▶ The cockpit today is much more ergonomic than it was just a decade ago, with many small changes to make the pilot's life easier.

◀ The latest generation of American fighters and bombers has seen an increase in stealth technology that includes changes to the weapons carried, in order to reduce the radar signature of the plane.

of-date combat fleets, although their economic situation is not particularly good. Chile took the first step, buying the F-16, also bought by Venezuela, and Brazil and Argentina are considering the same aircraft, if they can afford it.

The Asian market is seen as potentially very rewarding Apart from some countries which are trying to develop their own technology, the emerging economies of the region are searching for the best technology with which to defend themselves against the uncertainties which affect this part of the world. Whatever the future holds, the "combat-tested" label which comes with most American aircraft is always an advantage when the bargaining over new contracts begins.

THE F-14 TOMCAT
NAVAL FIGHTER

◄ *The Tomcat has been the main US naval fighter for almost three decades and still has some years of useful life left.*

► *In recent years, the Tomcat has assumed new missions that include the launching of precision weapons against terrestrial targets.*

The Grumman F-14 was conceived for use on large aircraft carriers. Famous for their intervention in combat against Libyan Sukhoi planes in the Gulf of Sirte and for being the mainstay of the "Top Gun" school, where many American naval pilots were trained, the Tomcat is respected by its opponents due to its capacities and performance. One of its latest missions has been the precision bombing of surface targets during the Lasting Freedom campaign in Afghanistan.

Development

After the failure of the naval variant of the TFX (Tactical Experimental Fighter), the US Navy sanctioned the development of a navy interceptor designated as the VFX at the end of 1967.

Decision

Once Grumman's 303-60 design had been tested and various adaptations made, it was declared the winner of the contest on January 15, 1969, receiving the identification of F-14 Tomcat. The first prototype began testing at Calverton on December 14, 1970.

Orders were received for 497 models. The first batch of F-14A was allocated to the VF-124 Gunfighters Squadron of NAS Miramar; in 1973

a squadron was deployed on the Enterprise for operational qualification and some were deployed in the evacuation of Saigon during Operation Frequent Wind. Production finished in April 1987 after 558 model A planes had been manufactured. Seventy-nine – of which around 20 remain in operation – were bought by Iran, possibly with Israeli help, after the beginning of the embargo imposed after the downfall of the Shah.

Upgrading

1987 also saw the first flight of the model B, with improved avionics and powered by the General Electric F110-GE-400 engine. This resulted in the production of 38 new planes, the first of which was delivered on April 11

1988 and the last in May 1990. At the same time, conversion began of some A class planes which were initially designated as A+ but finally also as B.

Super Tomcat

Between March 23 1990 and July 20 1992, 37 new F-14D Super Tomcat were delivered, equipped with new missiles, cockpits suitable for night-fighting, advanced tactical information screens and AN/APG-71 radar. Eighteen older planes were also converted to this standard. Additionally, on some planes, extra anchorage was added to accommodate a TARPS (Tactical Air Reconnaissance Pod) which allows real-time information gathering and sending of digital images by means

Technical Characteristics: Model D	
Cost (in millions of dollars):	58
Size:	
Length	19,10 m
Height	4,88 m
Wingspan; wings extended	19,54 m
Wingspan; wings retracted	11,65 m
Wing area	52,49 m²
Weight:	
Empty	18.951 Kg
Maximum	33.724 Kg
Maximum external load	6.577 Kg
Internal fuel	7.348 Kg
External fuel	1.724 Kg
Engines:	Two General Electric F110-GE-400 turbofans with 12,230 kg of unit thrust
Performance:	
Ceiling	16.650 m
High-altitute speed	Mach 1,88
Low-altitude speed	Mach 0,72
Combat range	800 Km
Ferry range	2.965 Km
Design load factor	7,5 g´s

of a coded radio link to any ship or ground station equipped with the Link 11 system.

Naval fighter

A squadron of F14 Tomcats is deployed on each US aircraft carrier, forming the base of combat air patrols (CAP) and acting as the long-range interception force. The F-14, in spite of its longevity is still considered a potent fighter and of the 710 planes constructed, 323 are still on active service, while some are stored in long-term availability conditions at the Mountain Home Air Base in Arizona.

Advanced design

The Tomcat is highly suitable for interceptor duties, as the angle of the wings can be varied between 20° and 68°. For naval deployment there is a robust landing gear with a launch bar on the front wheel and a brake hook which is caught by the arrester wire during landing, as well as a retractable nozzle for in-flight refueling Positioned at the rear, just below the two large tail units and the hydraulic airbrake, the two

The Tomcat is a fighter interceptor with excellent performances thanks to their two efficient turbines, their design and their wing capacity.

The F-14 can re-fuel in flight using other navy planes or tankers from other services or countries. Here, the fuel exchange is between two naval planes.

General Electric F110-GE-400 engines provide 24,260 kg of thrust.

Shared tasks

The cockpit has various side instrument panels and analogue and digital screens in the front. The copilot or RIO(Radar Intercept Officer) has a large circular TSD (Tactical Situation Display) that offers a detailed view of the tactical situation.

Avionics

The older Tomcats have a powerful Hughes AN/AWG-9 radar, able to detect targets at distances of up to 300 km and acquire 24 targets and engage 6, while the newer Tomcats include the AN/APG-71 Doppler radar with greater processing capacity, reliability and emission strength.

Armament

All the Tomcats carry a 20mm General Electric M61A1 gun and a combination of missiles including 4 short-range, infrared AIM-9 Sidewinder, four medium-range radar-guided AIM-7 Sparrow, and 6 long-range AIM-54C+ Phoenix able to intercept objectives within a radius of about 150 km. Additionally, many planes have been modified, with the designation of Bomcat, and these can carry out attack missions with weapons which include CBU-59 and Rockeye cluster bombs, laser-guided GBU-16 and 24, and anti-radar AGM-88 Harm missiles.

They are due to be fitted with SLAM launching capacity, derived from the anti-ship Harpoon and designed to reach reinforced targets within enemy territory.

F-15 EAGLE
ATTACK FIGHTER

Considered as the most advanced multi-role fighter in service, the F-15 has a record of over a hundred combat victories with none being shot down.

Evolved design

The well-known capacities of the Soviet interceptor MiG-25 led the United States to program, in 1965, the construction of a plane to combat it.

After evaluating the proposals of three corporations, on December 23 1969, McDonnell Douglas were contracted to build 18 single-seaters and 2 two-seaters for experimental tests, with the first of the YF-15A single-seaters having its first flight on July 27 1972 and the first of the two-seaters in July of the following year.

Contract

The first of the 572 planes of the production variant A/B contracted was delivered in November 1974 and the last in 1979. The same year, the first of a series of almost 500 improved planes, designated with the letters C/D and carrying 907kg of additional fuel had its first flight.

A commercial production agreement was signed with the Japanese firm Mitsubishi. The first of the two hundred Japanese F-15J/DJ was ready on August 26 1981. These planes include specifically-designed radar and electronic warfare systems which are not as good as the American equipment, although their performance has improved.

Multi-role

Two hundred two-seat E planes were built between 1988 and 1996.

Constructed for all-weather precision attacks, the Strike Eagle, as it was designated, integrates a synthetic aperture radar which offers better terrain-following, a FLIR infrared seeker, a Martin Marieta LANTIRN navigation and attack system, configured by the AN/AAQ-13 navigation and AN/AAQ-14 attack pods, and a rear cabin with 4 screens which share the work among the crew of two.

Exports

A specifically-designed export model, initially designated the H, has been purchased from 1994 by Israel with the code F-15I and by Saudi Arabia as the F-15S. To test ideas for future models and compete with the aggressive Russian export policy, a modified F-15B was built under the aegis of the STOL/MTD (Short Take Off and Landing/Maneuver Technology

◀ *The Eagle has evolved from its conception as an interceptor with a wide range of action to become a powerful multi-role fighter-bomber.*

▼ *The Eagle is one of the most advanced current fighter-bombers and is used by the air forces of the United States, Israel, Saudi Arabia and Japan.*

Demonstrator),equipped with two engines with jet nozzles that can be oriented in two axes and advanced reversed thrust, providing ultra-short landing capabilities.

Advanced

More than 1200 Eagles of types A , B, C, D and E have been acquired by the US. Air Force, with about 750 remaining on front-line duty, in the Reserve or being using by the National Guard. Boeing will deliver the last ten F-15E to the USAF between June 2002 and 2004. The production line will continue to manufacture the dozens of F-15K purchased in 2002 by South Korea and more orders are forecast.

Structure

The Eagle's optimized aerodynamics allows it to fly at high speeds at high altitudes and its Lear Astronics redundant digital flight control provides capacity for missions of automatic ground control.

The tricylcle landing gear has three single wheels and oleo-pneumatic shock absorbers to improve operating capabilities on temporary landing strips.

The twin tails, the large aileron in the centre of the upper part and two swept-back wings complete a design which makes the Eagle a formidable air-to-air combat plane.

Power

The two engines are located close to each other on the central axis enabling the plane to fly without problems if one engine fails. The Pratt & Whitney F-100-PW-220 turbofans were substituted after 1991 by the 229 engine that provides 12,200 kg of thrust per unit with afterburners. This permits very short takeoffs and an almost vertical climb at a speed of 15,000 m/minute.

Threats

The Eagle's exceptional combination of advanced systems gives it unequalled power against any air threat. The Hughes Aircraft AN/APG-70 Doppler radar which operates on band X in the fighter model and in band I in the attack plane, can acquire and engage targets up to 150 km away, as shown by the shooting down of four MiG-29 during the Balkans campaign and 33 Iraqi planes in 1991.

The ACES II zero-zero type ejector seat which can be launched at any altitude gives the pilot excellent rear and front visibility.

Missions

F-15 C, fighter-bomber	F-15 E, attack plane
Combat air patrols	Defense and superiority
Defense and superiority	Nuclear attack
Long range interception	Air-to-surface attack with bombs and missiles
Anti-satelite attacks (ASAT)	Cruise missile defense, ballistic missile defense (TDM) suppression of air attack defenses, reconnaissance. Undergoing testing

Technical Characteristics: Model C

Cost (in millions of dollas):	55	
Size:		
Length	19,45	m
Height	5,65	m
Wingspan	13,05	m
Wing area	56,50	m²
Flap area	3,33	m²
Weight:		
Empty	20.411	Kg
Maximum	36.700	Kg
Maximum external load	10.705	Kg
Internal fuel	6.103	Kg
External load	9.817	Kg
Engines:	2 Pratt & Whitney F100-PW-220 turbofans with 13,154 kg of unit thrust	
Performance:		
Ceiling	18.300 m	
High-altirude speed	Mach 2,5	
Low-altitude speed	Mach 1,21	
Take-off requirement	274 m	
Combat range	1.200 Km	
Ferry range	5.745 Km	
Design load factor	9 g's	

The General Electric M61A1 20 mm gun, with a magazine of 512 cartridges, the 4 infrared AIM-9 Sidewinder missiles and the raider-guided AIM-7 Sparrow and AIM-120 AMRAAM missiles of which 4 and 8, respectively, can be carried are the main air-to-air combat weapons.

Air-to-surface attacks are controlled by the Dynamics Control Corporation AN/AWG-27 arms control system which can manage missiles ranging from the AIM-65 Maverick precision missiles to B61 tactical nuclear bombs.

Defense measures include an automatic Northrop Grumman AN/ALQ-135(V) system of electronic countermeasures, a Magnavox AN/ALQ-128 radar alert system, RWR Loral AN/ALR-56C equipment and a Tracor AN/ALE-45 interference flare launcher.

The armament has been improved in recent years with the adaptation of systems such as the AGM-130 missile which, as it weighs 2,000 pounds can only be carried by the F-15E, and the JSOW, a bomb guided by in-flight satellite information.

F-16 FIGHTING FALCON,
THE MULTI-ROLE

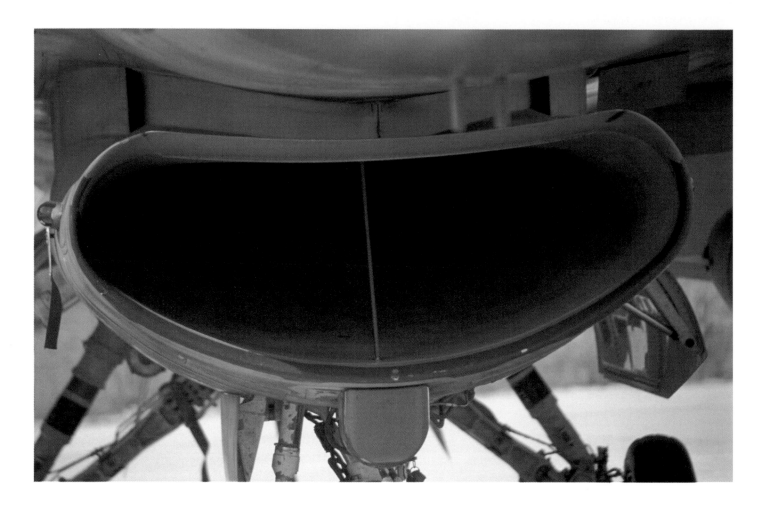

Initially conceived as a plane that would be simple to operate, economic and with advanced performance, the General Dynamics F-16 Fighting Falcon, in all its more than one hundred variants, has been a marked success, with more than 4,000 planes in service in more than twenty countries.

Light fighter

The U.S. Air Force LWF (LightWeight Fighter) program proposed the construction of a daylight light fighter with aerial superiority to complement the sophisticated F-15. The resulting prototype YF-16 first flew on February 2 1974.

Testing

The test flights of the pre-production models of the single-seat A F-16 and the two-seat F-16B were carried out between December 1976 and June 1978. Denmark, Holland and Norway decided to manufacture the plane under license.

Production

The A model, in 1978, began a production line which, with additional development programs is still manufacturing planes. The main client is the USA, who have more than 2,300 planes shared between the USAF, the Reserve and the National Guard, hundreds of which are in long-term storage. In 1984, the C variant(batch 25) introduced substantial changes in the cockpit and the structure. Between 1986 and 1992 the ADF program employing medium-range guided missiles was introduced and deliveries began of batch 40/42, the Night Falcon and batch 50/52, which two years later was equipped with Harm missiles and rede-

signated as the 50D/52 D. At the same time, the turbines were improved and upgraded and more than 300 USAF and NATO planes underwent an MLU (Mid Life Update) program lasting to 1999, with some forty planes being modified and redesignated as QRC (Quick Reaction Capability), in 1995, to operate in Bosnia. In 2001, Israel presented the ACE (Avionics Capabilities Enhancement) model with underwing fuel deposits of 600 gallons which substantially increases the plane's ability to carry out missions deep in enemy territory.

Customers

Besides the US.Air Force and the US.Navy – which uses the plane for training –, the Falcon has been purchased by Israel, Greece, Portugal, Belgium, Holland, Norway, Turkey, Bahrain, Venezuela, Egypt, South Korea, Thailand, Indonesia, Singapore, Pakistan and Taiwan. More countries, such as the United Arab Emirates, Italy, Chile and Oman intend to purchase the plane. In addition, Pakistan demanded, in 2002, the return of the 28 F-26 embargoed by the USA in 1990, as compensation for their support during the Afghanistan campaign in 2001. Second-hand planes are being offered to the former Warsaw Pact countries.

Excellence

The spectacular sales of the F-16 are a consequence of its versatility, endorsed by an excellent combat record in air-to-air or air-to-surface missions. The latest upgrade incorpo-

rates CFT tanks in the fuselage, which provide greater autonomy and longevity. The aim is to maintain the plane in service until beyond 2020 in the USAF and 2030 in other countries.

Cockpit
A feature of the cockpit is the polycarbonate canopy, which is covered by a fine layer of gold to reduce the frontal radar signature by around forty percent as well as providing an excellent field of vision. The McDonnell Douglas ACES II ejector seat is inclined 30° to improve the crew's tolerance of the high G-forces that are suffered during maneuvers.

Design
The wing configuration favors directional stability under extreme flight conditions. A single Pratt & Whitney F100-PW-220 or General Electric F110-GE-100 engine powers the plane by means of an unusual fixed air intake under the fuselage which ensures air flow at acute angles of attack, although when operating from unprepared runways there is a danger of sucking up foreign bodies.

Capacity
The plane has an in-flight refueling system and a tricycle landing gear whose front ele-ment retracts forward over the ventral struc-ture covering the air intake and the engine and backward-retracting back wheels.

The plane has a hook that engages the arrester wire for emergency landings. It is equipped with Tracor ANE-40/47 interfer-ence flare launchers, electronic warfare systems, Loral AN/ALR-56M radar alert systems, Magnavox AN/ARC-164 UHF Have Quick cypher communications equipment and connections for electronic warfare pods which can house the Westinghouse AN/ALQ-131 or AN/ALQ-184 reconnaissance systems.

F-18 HORNET
THE MULTI-ROLE

The F-18 was conceived as a cheap, light fighter. The development of a naval model showed its potential as a multi-role aircraft and dispelled any doubts as to its potential. During more than three million flying hours, the Hornet has beaten safety, operational, maintenance and mission capability records, resulting in many sales and continuous production, which is forecast to continue during the coming decade.

Development

In the Spring of 1974, the U.S. Navy published the requirements of the VFAX program which aimed to construct a low-cost, multi-role light fighter. The Navy was obliged by Congress to consider the General Dynamics YF-16 and Northrop YF-17 prototypes being evaluated by the USAF.

During the comparative studies, McDonnell Douglas, with the participation of Northrop, proposed a variant designated as the F-17, which was chosen as the naval model and identified as the NACF (Navy Air Combat Fighter). The fighter model was renamed as

the F-18 and the attack model as the A-18, but it was decided that the intermediate variant F/A-18 could carry out both roles without problems, being designated as the F-18 and named the Hornet.

Prototype

The first of a total of eleven YF-18 prototypes had its first flight on November 18 1978. After testing on aircraft carriers, the first F-18A was delivered to the U.S. Navy in May 1980 and the first operational squadron, which included type B two-seats was incorporated two years later.

Advanced versions

Between 1986 and 1987, the F-18C combat single-seat and the D two-seat combat/trainer was produced. In May 1988 the Night Attack model, basically the C/D model with improved avionics to enable 24-hour all-weather precision attacks entered production. In 1991, a bigger, more capable version designated as the F-18E/F Super Hornet was proposed. The prototype first flew on November 29 1995. Production of the first twelve of a scheduled 548 planes, to be delivered by 2010, began in 1997.

The improvements, already combat-tested,

included greater armaments and range of action, a reduced radar signature, exceptional
maneuverability in close combat and adaptation for ground attack. Currently, the two-seat
EA-18 AEA (Airborne Electronic Attack)F-18G Growler, is under construction.

Clients

The US. Navy and Marines have purchased the majority of Hornets constructed, although
the plane has also been sold to Canada, Australia, Malaysia, Finland, Kuwait, Switzerland
and Spain who purchased 72 planes under the aegis of the FACA program as well as 24
second-hand models.

Characteristics

Manufactured by McDonnell Douglas the F-18 can act as either an air defense fighter or a
precision attack plane. Both the single-seat and two-seat models feature a cockpit that is
ergonomic, comfortable and completely pressurized. It is equipped with three digital CRT

screens, frontal HUD and Martin-Baker SJU-5/6 ejector seats.

The two double-flow General Electric turbojets can go from normal speed to maximum afterburn in only 3 or 4 seconds.

To guarantee flying times, current models are fitted with internal fuel tanks of 6,061 L and three wet points under the wings for auxiliary tanks of 1,250 or 1,810 L, while the F model can handle almost 2 thousand liters of additional fuel.

Capacity

The Hornet's multi-role capabilities in air-to-air or air-to-surface combat are ensured by the rapid acceleration of the engines and the Hughes AN/APG-65 or 73 multimode digital radar, able to detect targets almost a hundred km away.

The robust landing gear, designed to be used on aircraft carriers, can be used on emergency runways. Its retractable outer sections allow easy check-ups and storage. The retractable nozzle located on the front upper fuselage permits in-flight refueling The equipment includes BITE (Built In Test Equipment) that reduces maintenance tasks considerably in general and the location of breakdowns in particular.

Armament

Depending on the model, the 9 or 11 external anchorage points allow 7 to 8 tons of weapons to be carried.

These include short-range AIM-9 Sidewinder and ASRAAM air-to-air missiles, medium-range AIM-7 Sparrow or AIM-120 AMRAAM missiles and the multi-barrel Vulcan M61A1 gun which can fire up to 4,000 shots per minute.

For ground attacks, the plane is armed with a variety of weapons including free-falling Mk82, Mk83 and Mk84 bombs and AGM-65 Maverick precision missiles, AGM-88 Harm antiradar missiles, AGM-84 Harpoon anti-ship missiles and SLAM multi-role missiles and B57 tactical nuclear bombs.

▲ *Precise attack is one the best qualities of the F-18.*

◀ *The Super Hornet is one of the latest generation of fighters and the US. Navy hopes to keep it operative for thirty years or more.*

TECHNOLOGICAL
RENEWAL

Recent advances in special materials, integrated electronics, sensors, etc., have led to a renewal of the technologies used to design and manufacture the new generation of fighter-bombers.

New potential

The aim of all companies is to maximize the manufacture of more sophisticated models with greater capacity while reducing both the price and maintenance costs.

Stealth capacity

A clear example of this tendency are the programs which aim to reduce the radar or thermal signature and even the level of noise produced by the engines. Research is ongoing on materials able to absorb radar waves or reflect them using special coverings or secret types of paint. In addition, every detail is calculated minutely and the best use made of current knowledge of cybernetics.

One result is that planes are less stylized. The wing inserts, the air intakes and the exhaust nozzles combine roundness with angularity, according to the demands of functionality. A totally blind radar signature may still be a pipe-dream, but planes like the Rafale or the Typhoon are not far from achieving it, often being confused with birds in flight.

More efficient sensors

Synthetic aperture radar, passive infrared sensors, safer cyphers, active systems of electronic interference, towed lures to interfere with the seeker heads of incoming missiles and a wide range of improved detection, invisibility and safety systems give a hint of the future electronic warfare.

More destructive

The new types of air-to-air and air-to-surface missiles are also undergoing a revolution. The efficacy of air-to-air missiles is based on their ability to make sharp turns at high speed in order to follow the target and to engage over-the-horizon targets, also a characteristic of air-to-surface missiles. The new cruise missiles can be launched from planes and automatically target objectives up to 400 km away, and can spread their smart bombs over specific areas. The aim is to keep the planes safe from the enemy, who must concentrate on shooting down the missiles.

THE JSF,
THE PLANE OF THE FUTURE

After the restructuring of various American military aircraft development programs dating from the 1980s, the Defense Advanced Research Projects Agency (DARPA) authorized a more-ambitious common development program which aimed to take advantage of the investment already made. The result was the Joint Strike Fighter (JSF), conceived to satisfy the needs of the Airforce, Navy and Marines with one plane. Other countries have joined the project and more than 3000 planes are forecast to be built by 2020.

Shared program

The idea was for a basic design which could be developed in various ways and would substitute both the Marine AV-8B Harrier and the ill-fated Navy A/F-X project, designed to replace the A-12 Avenger II, but which never progressed further than the design stage. The ASF project was first supported by the Navy and the Marines and later by the Airforce, each with clear ideas of the specific requirements that each branch would need.

Industrial plans

The project began life as the Joint Advanced Fighter (JAF). The enormous costs involved meant the formation of consortia to bid for the contracts. The Defense Department indicated its support for the project by canceling other programs such as the Multi-Role Fighter (MRF) and reducing orders for planes like the F-16 and F-18.

On January 27 1994, the Program Office was established. The first tasks were to agree the general nature of the plane: a single-engine, single-seater using composite materials and with a minimum radar signature. The project cost was estimated at more than 200 billion dollars, which would include the construction of the X-35A basic prototype which would be replaced by the fighter version, and the naval X35-C, and X-35B short take-off vertical landing (STOVL) prototypes. The three models would share 70-90% of parts and would thus be more economical than other models, even those they were designed to replace.

Competing proposals

Initial projects were received from Boeing, Lockheed Martin, McDonnell Douglas, and Northrop Grumman, whose very different designs had all been validated with wind-tunnel models.

The contest for the engine was between the Pratt & Whitney F119 and the General Electric YF120.

Choosing and evaluating the prototype

At the beginning of 1996, the project name was changed to JSF and the two winners of the competition were announced as Boeing and Lockheed Martin. Both companies, in consortia with other firms, received an initial contract of 1,100 million dollars for the Concept Development (CDF) phase, which involved the evaluation of prototypes using dynamic tests and was envisaged to be completed by the year 2000. Manufacturing previsions were for 1763 planes for the USAF, 609 for the Marines, 480 for the Navy and 150 for the Royal Navy and Royal Air Force. There was also great interest from other countries such as Canada, Holland, Israel, Italy and Turkey.

Delays in the project

The time-scale for the validation of prototypes of the three models was fulfilled with only slight delays, caused by the determination of the future buyers to ensure the performance and possibilities of their particular models. On October 26 2001, the winner of the competition was announced as the Lockheed Martin X-35; the Boeing X-32 was also considered highly satisfactory but somewhat more risky. The System Development and Demonstration (SDD) phase then began and is scheduled to continue until 2008, when the first planes should be ready. Lockheed Martin, in consortium with BAE Systems of the United Kingdom were awarded almost 19 billion dollars to complete the development and Pratt & Whitney Military Engines 4 billion dollars to complete the variants of the F119 engine.

Shared tasks

The winning consortium undertook to build 14 flight-ready planes and 6 or 7 for ground-testing The first plane should be ready by 2005 and the others by 2008. At present, manufacture will begin with the planes destined by the

◀ No two-seat trainer versions of the JSF are contemplated. Instead, complex simulators will be used.

▼ More than half a dozen countries have already shown interest in the JSF X-35, even though it is only at the prototype stage.

Marines and will continue, from 2012 onwards, with those for the USAF, followed by those for the Navy and for the UK Armed Forces. Holland has decided to participate in the second level. Poland is negotiating a collaborative effort for its new combat aircraft. Canada will buy the plane to replace its F-18. Australia is studying the industrial incentives on offer for its own project, the Air 6000. Norway has also shown interest and Israel will also benefit, firstly through the extensive participation of the Elbit company and later with the purchase of hundreds of planes.

Advanced specifications

The main characteristics of the X-35 are: a shape determined by stealth considerations; a combination of advanced composite materials which reduce weight, increase rigidity and reduce costs; increased cockpit visibility; high-resolution, long-range, highly-accurate synthetic aperture radar; cypher communications systems with data integration; advanced safety features; the weaponry, which includes air-to-air missiles and two 2,000lb guided bombs as well as an internal 27mm Mauser gun; long-range capabilities, especially the naval version which equals the F-18C; low fuel consumption at high speeds; the short take-off and landing capabilities; and, redundant processor management.

▲ In-flight refueling will extend the plane's range of action even more.

◄ Testing, which included coast-to-coast flights over the USA, confirmed the autonomy of the plane.

► The combination of shape, stealth capabilities, power and capacity make the JSF a shining example of aeronautical engineering.

THE NEW GENERATION
OF AIR-TO-GROUND WEAPONS

△ Guided missiles such as the French Martel combine high safety margins with great accuracy.

Only with the advent of the Vietnam War, with the use of the first precision-guided weapons, were great advances made in the capacity of air attacks to reach all targets. Since then there has been a continuous evolution, with both the Falklands War and the Gulf War showing that air power is essential to maintain total superiority.

Guns

Most fighter-bombers use both light machine-gun pods, firing either medium caliber 7.62x51mm (.308 Winchester) or heavy caliber 12.70x99mm, and guns integrated in the structure such as the American multi barrel Vulcan 20 and 30 mm, the German multi-barrel 27 mm, and the Swiss, Russian and French 30mm guns.

Free fall and submunitions

These include bombs of many types: conventional; low-resistance(more aerodynamic);bombs with integral parachutes; delayed action bombs which allow the bomber to distance itself from the explosion; braked-accelerated bombs with a rocket that ignites just before impact, anti-runway bombs for airbases, incendiary bombs containing highly inflammable material such as napalm; air combustible bombs which are highly explosive; and, cluster bombs containing various types of submunitions.

The most famous and most copied are the American Mk family, but there are many others including the Egyptian Kadar, the many varieties of Spanish Expal, the French Durandal, BAP and BL, the Yugoslav FAB, the Chilean WB, the Iraqi KAAKAA Iraqis, and the Russian

To guarantee pilot safety, these types of pods have been designed which are launched and guided independently to the target from hundreds of km of distance.

Betab AO/Aokh. In a class of its own is the American BLU-82 6,800 kg bomb transported in a MC-130H Hercules and nicknamed the Daisycutter in the recent Afghan conflict due to its destructive effects.

Submunitions are small explosive devices, mines or other artillery which, using bombs, fixed or self-propelled pods are spread over a large area in order to cause widespread damage. There are many models on the market, including the British Damocles and BL755 ,the French BLG66 Belouga,the German MW-1, the American CBUs and JSOW,the Chilean CB, the Russian KMG-OR , the South African CB470 and the Spanish BME 330.

Guided bombs

The system of bombs guided by laser or by electro-optics, proven in Vietnam and maintained in today's more advanced and accurate models, consists of installing a guide head in the nose of the bomb and a system of piloting in the fins. The target can be illuminated by the bombardier in the rear of the plane, a spotter infiltrated by land, an autonomous pod, or another plane,

using a signal which the bomb captures and follows to the point of impact. Currently, there are many models available including the American BLU-109/B, the French LGB 400 and 1,000 kg, the Israeli Griffin, Pyramid and Guillotine, the Russian KAB-500L, and the American Paveway III family which includes the GBU-24, 27 and 28.

Recent years have seen new systems of guidance introduced, such as the American MK-82 GPS Guided Taikit and Mk-84 GATS/GAM which both include a GPS (Global Position System)receiver which captures the deviation of the bomb from the target and gives the necessary corrections. Another curious development is the South African BARF (Booster Anti Radar Bomb)which contains a 250 kg Mk82 bomb combined with a seeker with passive raider and a system of mobile fins to direct the bomb to the target.

The JDAM bomb provides an economical, accurate option. Equipped with mobile fins and a GPS system, they require no illumination of the target previous to launching and can be launched from high altitudes to increase the range.

Specialized missiles

For specific or multi-role missions there is a comprehensive range of missiles that are equipped with an adaptable explosive warhead, a cruiser engine with sufficient fuel for 100 km in normal models and many thousands in cruise missiles, and a guidance system that can acquire targets and read the terrain.

▼ The latest generations of air-to-surface weapons are known as "smart bombs" as they can acquire,engage and destroy targets autonomously.

The general models include the American AGM-65 Maverick, Harpoon Block II with a warhead containing submunitions, SLAM and SLAM ER, the Argentinean Martin Pescador, the Swedish RB05, the French AS 30L, the Russian AS-7 Kerry, ACE-10 Karen, ACE-14 Kedge, Kh-25L and Kh-29L. Dedicated anti-ship missiles include the German Kormoran 2 ,the British Sea Eagle and Sea Skua ,the Israeli Gabriel, the French Exocet, the American AGM-84 Harpoon, the Swedish RBS 15, the Norwegian AGM-119 Penguin, the Russian X-15C, X-31 and X-35, and the Italian Mars 2.

Antiradar missiles include the British ALARM, the French Martel, the South African BARB, the Russian ACE-9 and X-25M, and the American AGM-88 HARM (High Speed Anti-Radiation Missile), of which a new, improved model is already available.

The nuclear option

In modern warfare, the use of both nuclear bombs and missiles with nuclear warheads is contemplated for both tactical and strategic objectives. Nuclear bombs include the American B61 and B83, while the missiles include the French ASMP, the various types of American cruise missiles and the advanced Russian models.

Capacity of air-to-surface weapons

Weapon	Targets
Gun, usually 20, 27 or 30 mm	Relatively unprotected targets such as convoys of lorries, light armored vehicles, fuel depots, control centers, etc.
Rockets	Used in salvos they can saturate a large area and are devastating against lightly-protected troops or vehicles.
Submunitions dispensers	Launch small bombs or anti-motion mines causing multiple impacts. Useful against poorly-protected targets or to halt the advance of infantry.
Free-fall bombs	Usually from 125 to 1000 kg, they have an explosive charge in a metal body and are used against lightly-protected targets.
Anti-runway bombs	Designed to put runways completely out of action.
Guided bombs	Using laser illuminators or optic systems, these bombs have a guided warhead which give a precision which lets them enter a window of 1.5x1.5 m.
Guided missiles	Controlled by the plane's radar or infrared systems these medium-range weapons can destroy targets where accuracy is vital such as bridges, shelters, ships, etc.
Anti-radar missiles	Locate enemy radar emissions and destroy both the radar and the anti-air defenses.
Anti-ship missiles	Using autonomous self-guiding systems, these missiles can reach ships at a range of 100km and destroy a ship of 4,000 tons.
Nuclear weapons	Usually tactical weapons which combine missiles and free-fall bombs with small atomic warheads.

◀ *The range of action of a bomber depends on its weight and the tendency is to use few, but very accurate weapons.*

▼ *Air-to-surface attacks using guided weapons has become more effective, with minimal margins of error.*

STEALTH
TECHNOLOGY

Following the research carried out in 1962 by the Soviet scientist Pyots Ufimtsev, the American Air force began, in 1974, evaluations managed by the DARPA (Defense Advanced Research Projects Agency), on the possibilities of building an aircraft that would be invisible to radar.

Conception

The XST program to develop a low-visibility plane was awarded to the Lockheed company, which had already built the SR-71 Blackbird spy plane. The Special Developments Division worked, from 1975 onwards, on the design of the shapes necessary to deflect radar waves and on the materials necessary to absorb them. Flying at night, and with the adequate screening of the engine exhaust it was considered that it would be very difficult to locate and intercept them.

Testing

Using a scale model to test the performance of the design inside an anechoic chamber, and another full-size model to measure the real results obtained, it proved possible to construct a model which generated an echo one thousand times smaller than normal aircraft. The positive results encouraged the building of two prototypes of the Have Blue, the first of which flew for the first time in December 1977.

After the tests, 5 pre-production models were ordered, the first of which took off on June 18, 1981 from the secret Tonopah Base in the Nevada desert. Fifty-nine production models followed, for which allocations were made in the 1980-1988 budgets.

Stealth

The existence of the F-117A Black Jet, as it was named until the official designation of Night Hawk, was systematically denied by the U.S. Air Force until November 1988 when the first pictures were published and details became known. The last plane was delivered on July 12 1990 and the first shooting down occurred on March 27 1999 while carrying out a bombing raid on the former Yugoslavia.

F-117A Night Hawk

At present, around fifty F-117A remain on active service, deployed in the 7th , 8th and 9th squadrons of the 49th Fighter Wing at Holloman Base in New Mexico.

Advanced

The shape of the Lockheed Martin Skunk

Works F-117 represents a radical break with previous conceptions of aerodynamic lines. The planes are covered with RAM material which absorbs radar waves, giving them a radar section estimated at 0.01 per square meter.

The Skunk Works has severe delta wings, a double vertical tail, air intakes integrated with the fuselage and covered by a fine grid, air intakes integrated in the fuselage and covered by a fine grid, exhaust nozzles which incorporate heat-reflecting ceramic tiles similar to those developed for NASA's Space Shuttle program, and a cockpit whose canopy is not rounded and which is composed of transparent panels covered with a fine layer of gold to dissipate heat.

However, there were problems with stability which were solved using an advanced, quadruple, digital GEC Astronics control system.

Cockpit

The cockpit has an ACES II ejector seat and advanced presentation and management systems that ensure satisfactory all-weather flying, even without radar. The equipment has been improved, with a new, more accurate flight control system, color screens, new IBM processors, improved software, digital situation screens, GPS systems and a new IRADS sensor to acquire and designate targets.

Guided

The weapons are guided using a stabilized infrared Texas Instruments FLIR/DLIR seeker which also includes a laser illuminator which will be substituted by the new IRADS. The normal cargo load is two laser-guided 907 kg BLU-109B or GBU-10/27 bombs.

Details

Small enough to be carried within a Galaxy transporter, the plane's fuselage is made of aluminum with titanium inserts around the engines and a polymer covering which includes magnetic particles.

Propelled by two General Electric F404-GE-F1D2 engines without afterburners, which deliver 4,900 kg of thrust per unit and were developed from those used for the F-18, the plane can achieve a cruising speed of 0.9 Mach with low fuel consumption.

The engines are fed by a tank integrated in the upper part of the fuselage, set back from the propulsion system, which gives the plane an autonomy of 2,268 km, which can be increased by using an upper tank, also integrated in the fuselage, for in-flight refueling.

F/A-22 Raptor

Initially conceived to complement and, eventually, substitute the F-15 Eagle, the choice of a new stealth fighter lay between the YF-22 and YF-23 designs, with the first, built

by Lockheed Martin Aeronautical Systems being chosen.

The YF-22 carried out its first flight on September 29, 1990. The complexity of its development led to some design faults; the auxiliary power unit failed, there was fuel loss, and the software was inadequate. The General US Accounting Office continues to have questions about the cost-efficiency ratio of the plane.

The first test F-22A Raptor – the evaluation model n° 4001 – came of the line on April 9 1997 at the Georgia plant, with the first test flight being carried out, after several delays, on September 7 1997, with the head test pilot, Paul Metz, at the controls.

Since then, several prototypes have been manufactured and the manufacture of the first pre-production series has been approved.

This will include over a dozen improvements, especially in the use of Block 3.0 software, compared with the original designs.

Service

With the EDM (Engineering and Manufacturing Development) evaluation in full flow, the US Air Force began to apply pressure to ensure the production of 339 planes, while other sectors of the administration were trying to reduce this figure to around 200. The increased defense budget announced in 2002 may lead to even more planes being built.

In the long term, the possible introduction of a two-seat attack plane is under consideration. This could be ready by 2012, when production of the A/B series finishes.

Advanced

The plane has been produced with advanced materials including titanium, aluminum, carbon fiber, steel and thermoplastics to guarantee its aerodynamic qualities and the smallest possible radar signature. The design includes a wing-formation that reduces the reflected signal with a diamond shape to increase fuel deposits, in-flight refuelling capabilities, swept-back air intakes and improved pilot vision and an integrated fiber-optic flight control system. The plane is powered by two Pratt & Whitney F-11-PW-100 turbines providing 15,890 kg of thrust. The engines include two-dimensional nozzles able to direct their exhaust gases at an angle of +/-20°. This provides the Raptor with great maneuverability and speeds of up to Mach 1.58 – supercruiser speed – without afterburners. Two central CIP (Common Integrated Processors) coordinate the sensors, connect the sophisticated integrated avionics systems, manage the flight while connecting with the radar to achieve optimum navigation and air-to-air combat. The armament, which is housed in 3 internal bays, includes short-range infrared Sidewinder missiles, medium-range laser-guided Amraam missiles and 454 kg bombs. The maximum interior load is 2,268 kg which can be augmented with the use of four external pods used for weapons or fuel. These specifications ensure that the F/A-22A will dominate the skies during the coming decades.

Technical Characteristics

	F-117A	F/A-22
Cost (in millions of dollars):	42,6	90
Size:		
Length	20,08 m	18,92 m
Weight	3,78 m	5,00 m
Wingspan	13,20 m	13,56 m
Wing area	105,9 m²	78m²
Flap area	---	5,10 m²
Weight:		
Empty	13.608 Kg	14.365 Kg
Maximum	23.813 Kg	27.216 Kg
Maximum load	2.268 Kg	2.268 Kg
Internal fuel	---	14.000 l (estimated)
External fuel	No	No
Engines:	2 General Electric F404-GE-F1D2 turbines without afterburners	2 Pratt & Whitney F119-PW-100 turbines with afterburners
Performance:		
Ceiling	---	15.240 m
High-altitude speed	Mach 1	Mach
Low altitude speed	Mach 0,9	Mach 1,3
Approach speed	227 Km / h	---
Combat range	1.112 Km	---
Ferry range	2.268 Km	---
Design load factor	+6 g´s	+9 g´s

◀ *The F-117 is difficult to detect and only one loss, over the former Yugoslavia, has been reported.*

▼ *The F-117 has a tricycle landing gear, similar to that of the F-16, with the front and back wheels folding forward and covered by flaps with shapes that decrease the signature radar.*

Photo Credits

Lockheed Martin:
6, 70, 71, 72, 73, 74, 75

Matra BAE Dynamics:
15, 40, 52

Mc Donell Douglas:
65, 66

Octavio Díez:
7, 8, 16, 18, 20, 22, 23, 24, 25, 26, 27, 28, 30, 31, 33, 34, 35, 36, 37, 38, 39, 46, 48, 49, 50, 53, 54, 57, 58, 59, 62, 64, 68, 69, 76, 76, 76, 77, 79, 83, 84, 85, 86, 87, 88

Saab-BAE:
41, 42, 43

US Navy:
32, 51

Remaining photographies:
Northrop Grumman, Alenia Aerospazio, Aerospatiale Matra, Alenia Marconi Systems, Lockheed Martin, McDonnel Douglas, Metra BAE Dynamics, Saab-British Aerospace, BAE Systems